Collective Biographies

WOMEN OF PEACE

Nobel Peace Prize Winners

Anne Schraff

ENSLOW PUBLISHERS, INC.

Bloy St. and Ramsey Ave.   P.O. Box 38
Box 777   Aldershot
Hillside, N.J. 07205   Hants GU12 6BP
U.S.A.   U.K.

Library of Congress Cataloging-in-Publication Data

Schraff, Anne E.
    Women of peace: Nobel Peace Prize winners/ Anne Schraff.
        p. cm. — (Collective biographies)
    Includes index.
    ISBN 0-89490-493-0
    1. Pacifists—Biography—Juvenile literature. 2. Nobel Prizes—Juvenile
literature. 3. Peace—Awards—Juvenile literature. [1. Pacifists. 2. Nobel Prizes.
3. Women—Biography.] I. Title. II. Series.
JX1962.A2S37 1994
327.1'72'0922—dc20
    [B]   93-37429
                                                                   CIP
                                                                    AC

Printed in the United States of America

10 9 8 7 6 4 3 2 1

Illustration Credits:
AP/Wide World Photos, pp. 46, 87, 103; Carolyn Gorny-Kopkowski
OSB/Pax Christi USA, p. 56; Library of Congress, pp. 8, 14, 27, 42; L.R.
Montali, Jr./The Southern Cross, pp. 58, 67; ©Nobel Foundation, pp. 82,
92; Papers of Emily Greene Balch, Swarthmore College Peace Collection,
p. 38; Schlesinger Library, Radcliffe College, pp. 20, 31, 34; United
Nations, pp. 70, 77.

Cover Illustration:
L.R. Montali, Jr./The Southern Cross

Contents

Preface   5

1 Baroness von Suttner: Peace Bertha . . .   9

2 Jane Addams: An Extremist for Peace . . 21

3 Emily Greene Balch:
   The Planetary Citizen 35

4 Mairead Corrigan and Betty Williams:
   Guerrillas for Peace 47

5 Mother Teresa: Saint of the Gutter . . . 59

6 Alva Myrdal:
   Conscience of Disarmament 71

7 Daw Aung San Suu Kyi:
   Heroine of the "Golden Land" 83

8 Rigoberta Menchu:
   To Share the Dream of Peace 93

   Chapter Notes 105

   Index 111

Preface

Throughout history, people have searched for peaceful resolutions to national problems. Women from many countries have played a role in this quest—especially since the early nineteenth century when women gained more power and influence over their own destinies. Most of the women who joined organizations for peace have been unsung heroes. But a few were recognized by the most prestigious honor—the Nobel Prize for Peace.

The first Nobel Prize for Peace was awarded in 1901 to recognize the most important work that year in advancing the cause of world peace. Since then, nine women have been named Nobel laureates. They have been very different kinds of women—young and old, married and single, holders of important international offices and ordinary people. And they have come from all over the world—Europe to Asia to North and South America.

Some of the women—such as Baroness Bertha von Suttner, Emily Balch, and Jane Addams—received the honor after long careers of working for peace in international organizations. These women drew considerable criticism for daring to oppose their nation's decision to go to war. For these women, the Nobel Peace Prize was a well-deserved recognition of a lifetime of labor in nonviolent resolutions of problems.

Others—such as the Irish laureates Mairead Corrigan and Betty Williams—were ordinary women occupied with the everyday concerns of family. They had no thoughts of dramatically changing the world. But violent events in their country thrust them into the role of peace activists.

Alva Myrdal, also a wife and mother, was honored after a long career as a diplomat and member of the United Nations (UN). When Mother Teresa won the award in 1979, new ground was broken. She was not recognized for membership in peace organizations or for efforts to stop any particular war. Her unique life's work among the poor led the Nobel Prize Committee to recognize the fact that many wars take root among abandoned and unloved peoples. Mother Teresa's transformation of poor people's lives was seen as a powerful act for peace.

The first Asian woman to receive the prize, Daw Aung San Suu Kyi, was recognized for struggling to achieve civil rights and democracy in her country. Rigoberta Menchu, a force for economic and civil justice in Guatemala, was recognized as a symbol for all South American people who have long suffered oppression.

In spite of the efforts of these valiant women, and many people like them, the world is still ravaged by war and injustice. Since the first Nobel Prize for Peace was awarded, millions have died in hundreds of wars. Between sixty and seventy million lives were lost in the two world wars alone! Many more millions have been wounded or made homeless and destitute by war. The major world powers have nearly been bankrupted by waging wars or preparing for armed conflict.

Still, through the efforts of these nine women and other good people all over the world, small—but important—first steps have been taken toward world peace. As long as women such as these nine continue to bring unity where there are divisions, justice where there are wrongs, and healing where there is suffering, we can take heart and follow their shining examples.

Baroness von Suttner

Baroness von Suttner

Peace Bertha

Martha was a young soldier's wife who became a war widow when her husband was killed in Italy. She married another soldier who shared her hatred of war. But out of a sense of duty and patriotism, he too went to the battlefield in 1864 and 1866. Finally, repelled by the horrors he witnessed, he resigned his military commission. He was shot on suspicion of being a Prussian spy during the Franco-Prussian War. This is the plot of the book *Die Waffen nieder! (Lay Down Your Arms)*,[1] which became the most famous anti-war novel of its time. Describing the sufferings of war, the book gained fame all over the world and was compared to *Uncle Tom's Cabin* as a powerful "novel with purpose."[2]

The author was Bertha Felicie Sophie Kinsky, Baroness von Suttner.

Bertha Kinsky was born in 1843 in Prague, Czechoslovakia, to a distinguished noble family. Her father was Count Franz Joseph von Kinsky, a general in the Austrian army. He, ironically, loved to regale his daughter with war stories. Despite its nobility, the family often lived in poverty. Bertha seemed destined for an uneventful life in such jobs as governess for the wealthier von Suttner family. But she had early literary ambitions and was drawn to intellectual debates about the social issues of the day. However, an ad in a Vienna newspaper changed her life.

Alfred Nobel, a Swedish inventor who lived in Paris, was in need of a cultured and mature woman to serve as his homemaker, secretary, and hostess. The forty-three-year-old Nobel had never married. He was also the inventor of dynamite and other destructive explosives on which he had built an industrial empire. It was Nobel's ad in the newspaper that thirty-three-year-old Kinsky read.

Going to Paris, the center of European cultural activity, would have appealed to any ambitious young woman. However, Kinsky had other motives as well. She had fallen in love with the son of her employers, Arthur Gundaccar von Suttner. Twenty-six-year-old Arthur von Suttner loved Kinsky as well, but his parents bitterly opposed his choice. So Kinsky went off to Paris to interview for Nobel's job.

Kinsky liked Alfred Nobel immediately. The two

were compatible and discussed topics both were interested in—literature, world affairs, and philosophy. They also shared a common outlook.[3] Nobel hired Kinsky, but she was on the job just one week when a frantic telegram from Arthur von Suttner came from Vienna. "I cannot live without you,"[4] he had written. Without a moment's hesitation, Kinsky left Nobel a note and rushed back to Vienna.

In 1876—against the furious protests of his family—Baron Arthur von Suttner took Bertha Kinsky to be his wife, who became Baroness von Suttner. The young man's family cut him off without a cent, sending the newlyweds into dire poverty. The couple moved to Tiflis in the Caucasus of Russian Georgia. There they made a meager living teaching languages and music to the children of nobility in the area.

When the Russo-Turkish wars—campaigns between Russia and the decaying Ottoman Empire—flared up again in 1877, the von Suttners saw close up the misery of war. They saw it in the scarred bodies of wounded soldiers and in the frightened faces of refugee families. Baron von Suttner wrote war reports and descriptive articles for German and Austrian papers. The baroness also wrote articles and stories. In fact, the outline of her powerful anti-war novel began to take shape in her heart and mind.

During this time Baroness von Suttner continued her correspondence with Alfred Nobel. Often they discussed a project by which Nobel could advance the cause of peace.

Baroness von Suttner finished her novel, *Lay Down Your Arms*, which was based on the horrors of European wars between 1859 and 1871. She sent it to a publisher who had used her magazine stories. The publisher returned the manuscript, saying that its readers would be offended by the graphic descriptions of war's cruelties.

Baroness von Suttner then sent the manuscript to a German book publisher who offered to buy it— providing the most horrifying passages were struck out. Baroness von Suttner, however, refused to change a word. The publisher reluctantly published the book anyway, all the while dreading the reaction of the German reading public. To the publisher's surprise, the book was received enthusiastically and became an overnight success. By 1914 the book had gone through forty editions and had been translated into sixteen different languages. Baroness von Suttner sent Nobel a copy, and he warmly congratulated her.

In 1885 von Suttner's family had at last become reconciled to his marriage. So von Suttner and his wife returned to Vienna, where the baroness wrote a second novel, *Das Machinezeitalter (The Machine Age)*. In this book she imagined a future of solidarity and peace among all nations. Soon after the novel's publication, the von Suttners visited Alfred Nobel in Paris. Baroness von Suttner had founded the Austrian Peace Society and she suggested Nobel might help its cause by donating money.

Nobel talked about some practical plan for peace by which nations would be compelled to accept a year of arbitration before going to war. Then Nobel and the baroness discussed the idea of an annual peace prize that might be awarded to the person or group who did the most to advance world peace. This prize, the two finally concluded, would be the most practical contribution to the cause of peace.

Now deeply involved in the peace movement, Baroness von Suttner traveled to Budapest, Hungary, in 1896 to attend the International Peace Congress. Unfortunately, news reached her there that her friend, Alfred Nobel, had died. However, she may have been consoled by the fact that the Nobel Peace Prize was already established and that Nobel's work would go forward.

War clouds were now gathering over the continent of Africa. From 1899 to 1902 the British would fight against the Boers (descendants of the original Dutch settlers) for control of South Africa. Eventually the British would win, but not before losing over twenty thousand men to battle injuries and disease. Baroness von Suttner said that the imperialistic policy behind the war was not the most dangerous aspect of the tragedy. The worst, she said, was that leaders were mobilizing man's noblest

Swedish inventor Alfred Nobel often discussed the idea of an annual peace prize with his friend, Bertha von Suttner.

instincts of self-sacrifice and concern for justice to back indefensible imperial schemes.[5]

Baroness von Suttner dreamed of the marvelous progress humankind could make if the idealism roused by war could be channeled toward peaceful projects.[6] She lectured all over Europe on this theme and hoped she and other crusaders were having an impact.

The outbreak of the Spanish-American War in 1898 was another bitter blow to those seeking a more peaceful world. Baroness von Suttner regarded the "New World" of America as more advanced and less likely to succumb to the temptation of war. Thus when conflict occurred there it was especially sad.

But then the Russian Czar Nicholas II called a conference of world representatives to consider ways to achieve world peace, and Baroness von Suttner applauded this act. German Emperor William II, however, took a less optimistic view of the idea of world peace conferences. He said, "Peace will never be better assured than by a thoroughly drilled army ready for instant action!"[7]

The First Hague Peace Conference in 1899 was a major event in Baroness von Suttner's life. She and her husband attended every session of the ten-week conference. One hundred delegates from twenty-six countries participated and decided to establish a permanent International Arbitration Court at the Hague.

Newspapers chronicling Baroness von Suttner's activities for peace nicknamed her "Peace Bertha."[8] Certainly the attractive, animated, fashionably dressed, ardent pacifist made a striking impact on the lecture circuit.

The first Nobel Peace Prize was about to be given in 1901. Jean Henri Dunant, a Swiss philanthropist who helped found the Red Cross, was chosen. Baroness von Suttner might well have expected to win the prize herself since she and Nobel consulted together in establishing it. But if she was disappointed, she acted graciously. Still von Suttner complained that Dunant tried to "humanize" war instead of end it. As she phrased it, "Sir George rode forth to kill the dragon, not to trim his claws."[9]

In 1902 Baron von Suttner died. He had been Bertha von Suttner's loving companion for twenty-six years, and his death was a grievous loss. The von Suttners' marriage was truly a love match achieved against great odds, and Baroness von Suttner might have gone into seclusion in her grief. Instead she continued her crusade for peace.

Now in her fifties and in good health, Baroness von Suttner lived alone in a Vienna apartment with little social life but relentless peace activism. In the fall of 1904 she crossed the Atlantic Ocean for the first time in her life to participate in a Boston peace conference. She had called America a true "New World" and expected that her message of peace would be well received. She was correct.

In the following year, as she toured Germany, the baroness was notified that she was to receive the 1905 Nobel Peace Prize. Baroness von Suttner would be the first woman to be given that honor. She must have been grateful for the recognition, and she badly needed the financial reward of the prize as well.

In her Nobel Prize address, Baroness von Suttner said, "Terrible warlike relapses may yet occur, but the future will confirm my faith: the peace of nations is on the way."[10]

Baroness von Suttner was now more than ever in demand as a lecturer. Her articles were published all over the world. In 1907 she attended the Second Hague Peace Conference, and her advice was solicited by many different corners of the world—even Peking, China, where she was invited to speak.

In 1912 Baroness von Suttner returned to America and was enthusiastically received everywhere she went. The Carnegie Endowment for International Peace gave her a monthly pension, which at last ended her lifelong struggle with intermittent poverty.

On her return to Europe, Baroness von Suttner saw the growing threat of yet another war. Now that nationalistic passions were again on the rise, she was not universally regarded as a benign figure. Austrian military men denounced her for speaking about peace and sapping the patriotism of a nation that might soon need to go to war. In some quarters she was called a traitor for speaking so vigorously on behalf of peace.

"It seems to me," Baroness von Suttner sadly wrote, "that the great European disaster is well on the way." Lamenting the stockpiled armaments, she said, "the gunpowder will soon explode."[11]

History was now proving her earlier optimistic visions of the future premature. Yet Baroness von Suttner continued her relentless crusade for peace. She warned against the danger of militarizing China, condemned the use of the airplane as a weapon of war, and pleaded for a united Europe as a guarantee of peace.

Word from America that a vigorous peace movement flourished there reached the baroness, and this news undoubtedly encouraged her. She was now past seventy years of age and her health was in decline. As she lay on her deathbed she continued to plead for peace. Memories of herself as a young woman writing the passionate anti-war novel recurred. In fact, her last comments were "Lay down your arms! Tell that to many, many people!"[12]

Baroness von Suttner died in June 1914—a week before the assassination of Archduke Francis Ferdinand, heir to the Hapsburg throne of Austria-Hungary. His assassination was the event that triggered World War I. Mercifully, Baroness von Suttner did not live to see the tragic events that unfolded, causing World War I. War was an outcome she had so tirelessly worked to prevent.

In a cruel irony, World War I provided a gruesome arena for the use of Alfred Nobel's modern explosives. Almost twenty million people were killed in World War I—many by those destructive explosives.

Jane Addams

Jane Addams

An Extremist for Peace

The slender, dark-haired, twenty-three-year-old American woman watched Bavarian women struggling to carry heavy casks of hot beer to cooling stations. Often the hot beer spilled, scalding their heads and shoulders. The women worked from 5:00 A.M. to 7:00 P.M. for about thirty-seven cents a day. The incident lived long in the heart and mind of this American tourist, Jane Addams.[1] The struggling Bavarian women were more evidence of the injustice and suffering she would see around the world and in America—evidence that would shape her many crusades, often as the lone champion of unpopular causes.

Jane Addams was born in 1860 in Cederville, Illinois. She credited her father, John Huy Addams, with wielding a powerful influence on her thinking.[2] A self-made man, he built a sawmill and a gristmill into a small fortune. But his major concern was building his community, attempting to improve prisons, insane asylums, and schools. His dark-eyed daughter learned well from his civic spirit.

Her mother, Sarah, died when Jane was just two years old. Older sisters then ran the household until John Addams remarried. Jane, or "Jennie" as she was called, was a sickly child, suffering from tuberculosis of the spine. This illness left her with a curved back, pigeon-toed walk, and a cocked angle to her head. Young Jennie was a quiet child who often lost herself in books. She attended a one-room school, and her grades were just average. Though her family was prosperous, Jennie played with the neighborhood children from all classes of society. By age sixteen she had become an attractive girl who ice skated. She also had a lively sense of humor that belied her sad looking eyes.

Jane Addams was one of the first generation of American college women. Prior to her generation, few girls went on to higher education. Thus Jane and her peers felt like pioneers. She attended Rockford School where the purpose of education was "to teach the great Christian lesson that the true end of life is not to acquire the most good but to give oneself for the good of others."

Addams' ill health continued to interfere with her plans after she finished college. She wasn't well enough to enter medical school as she planned, so she was sent to Europe to recover her vitality. In Europe, Addams climbed mountains, rode trains, and tramped through museums—growing vigorous. It was on this trip to Europe that she visited Toynbee Hall, a settlement house in London, England, that provided education and recreation for the poor. Addams and her friend, Ellen Gates Starr, had often talked about doing something similar for the poor in Chicago, Illinois. The idealistic young women now set out to realize their mutual dream.

In the spring of 1888, Addams and Starr chose a run-down house—the former Charles J. Hull mansion—to open what became the "Hull House," a meeting place for the neighborhood poor. She considered the Hull House a microcosm of the world, where members of different nationalities and classes learned to respect each other and live together.[3]

Soon neighborhood women came to Hull House, toting along their children. There was an opportunity for education and clubs for both boys and girls. Jane Addams gained the reputation of an angel of mercy and lady bountiful.[4]

Addams noticed that workers in nearby factories were being oppressed by long hours and unsafe conditions. So she became a mediator in labor disputes, always rejecting the most radical position. Yet in spite of her moderate stance, she was often accused of being too pro-labor or even socialistic. It was the beginning of a controversy that would dog her all her life.

Addams worried about the thousands of young men and women who had migrated from the safety of the farms to the crowded and dangerous city. Who would look after their futures, she asked. "Never before in civilization have such numbers of young girls been suddenly released from the protection of home and permitted to walk unattended upon city streets under alien roofs; for the first time they are being prized more for their labor than for their innocence."[5]

Addams also involved herself in the garbage problem in the Chicago slums. She was incensed at the filth caused by bakeries, slaughter houses, fruit peddlers, liverymen, and ordinary citizens just dumping their waste in the streets. Addams noted that even dead horses lay rotting in the open! City collection was haphazard and the stench, especially in warm weather, was unbearable.

Addams protested to city hall hundreds of times until, accompanied by two businessmen, she personally submitted a bid to clean up the neighborhood. Her bid was rejected, but she was appointed Garbage Inspector at an annual salary and she made some improvement in the cleanliness of the streets. The image of a determined five-foot-three-inch, one-hundred-pound lady campaigning against the entrenched power of city hall captured the imagination of the nation.

Addams was always an avid reader, whose reading list included the pacifist works of Russian novelist Leo Tolstoy. Although her father was a Quaker, she was not raised in a pacifist tradition. As a young woman touring Europe she showed no special horror at seeing battlefields or war memorials. But the Spanish-American War brought another turning point in her life.

On October 17, 1899, Addams listened to German-American reformer Carl Schurz denounce President William McKinley for the killing of Filipino civilians in the aftermath of the Spanish-American War. Addams began investigating what demands true patriotism made upon an individual. She came to the conclusion that patriotism meant service to the community—not just taking part in wars.

Addams attended many anti-war meetings and called for a "moral substitute for war," saying "War is a terrible thing. It is the law of the jungle."[6] But for several more years Addams' pacifism did not occupy much of her time, for she was kept very busy helping the children at Hull House.

Many new immigrants had come into the neighborhood and they needed safe places for recreation. The hard, mean streets swallowed young girls into prostitution and led boys into crime. So many youngsters were arrested for petty crimes and thrown into adult prisons that Addams campaigned for the first juvenile court in the nation. The court was designed to help youngsters straighten out, not to punish them and insure a criminal future. A major breakthrough in the treatment of juvenile offenders, the court eventually became the norm.

In 1910 Addams published *Twenty Years at Hull House,* the story of her work among the poor. Addams called Hull House a place where many worked for the good of all. She compared it to "a thousand voices singing the "Hallelujah Chorus" in Handel's *Messiah,* saying "it is possible to distinguish the leading voices, but the differences in training and cultivation between them and the voices of the chorus are lost in the unity of purpose."[7]

Jane Addams became world-famous as the driving force in efforts to improve the lives of millions of Americans. And in 1912, addressing the Progressive Party Convention, she reached the peak of her popularity. During this emotional convention she endorsed Theodore Roosevelt for President because his policies embraced many of her social programs. Addams was almost universally regarded as the saintly spokeswoman of all that was good in America—but all that was soon to change.

When World War I broke out in Europe, Jane Addams joined three thousand other women on January 10, 1915, in Washington D.C. The women gathered to demand an immediate convention of neutral nations to end the hostilities. The Women's Peace Party was established toward this purpose.

Subsequently, Addams and other peace activists traveled to the Hague, in the Netherlands, where

As World War I broke out in Europe, Jane Addams began her work as a peace activist.

Addams presided over the International Congress of Women. This Congress created the International Committee of Women for Permanent Peace, which tried to persuade the warring powers to restore peace. Addams was elected chair of this committee and during the next few months she traveled to various European capitals, pleading for peace.

Addams and her fellow pacifists viewed barricaded cities, bombed-out buildings, and wounded and maimed soldiers in hospitals. Most of the diplomats received her coolly, regarding this women's peace delegation almost with amusement. How could Addams and her cohorts believe they would get a serious hearing from men busy conducting a war?

When Addams returned to America later that year, she was greeted with criticism and derision. Theodore Roosevelt himself called her and the other women "hysterical pacifists," describing their mission as "silly and base." Roosevelt poked fun at Addams as "poor bleeding Jane" who was part of the "shrieking sisterhood." In a takeoff on his old Bull Moose party, he named Addams "bull *mouse*."[8]

Most Americans reacted to Addams' peace mission with a shrug and a smile. If she had quit her crusade at this point, she might have escaped the fury that was to come her way. Instead she pressed on. In a speech at New York's Carnegie Hall on July 9, 1915, she seemed to strike at the very heart of soldierly glory. She told the crowd that young men who were fighting didn't really want the war. Addams charged that it was the old and middle-aged who had decided the cause was righteous and that they would demand a fight to the bitter end without considering compromise.

In her most shocking allegation, Addams said that the average soldier is not "sufficiently brutish or beastly to fight with cold steel against his brother unless primed with drugs or strong drink."⁹ She told of a young Swiss soldier who said he went to the battlefield and deliberately misfired to avoid hitting an enemy because he couldn't live with himself if he took a life. She also described five young Germans who committed suicide rather than be forced to kill other soldiers.

A firestorm against Jane Addams sprang to life on both sides of the Atlantic. That she would dare suggest soldiers fighting in drug-induced stupors rather than inflamed with patriotism was unforgivable to many. Hate letters denouncing Addams as a "pitiful failure" and a "silly, vain impertinent old maid"¹⁰ poured into Hull House. Addams was accused of knowing nothing of the joy that soldiers find in fighting a just war. Friends who did not abandon Addams outright, for the most part, kept silent. But Addams refused to back down.

Near Addams fifty-fifth birthday, her health began to worsen. Some of her old problems resurfaced, and the pressures of going from America's most admired to most reviled woman were beginning to show. Still she visited President Woodrow Wilson to urge him to keep the United States from entering World War I. She pleaded with the President to use his influence to mediate the war and bring about peace. She thought that he was receptive to her ideas, but on April 2, 1917, President Wilson called for a declaration of war. America was now part of the war Addams loathed. Almost alone among the pacifists, she continued her opposition.

Addams was kept under surveillance by the Department of Justice, but she told her niece that her convictions were unwavering. She refused to rally around the cause of the war. Instead she tirelessly raised money for the relief of the war's starving victims.

After World War I, America entered a period of destructive suspicion of anything believed to be "un-American." There was disrespect for free speech, large-scale wiretapping of telephones, and roundups of aliens suspected of disloyalty. In this atmosphere, pacifists were often denounced as communists. When Addams was called a communist she replied, "I am a pacifist, but I have been loyal to my country."[11] Still, the Lusk Committee, established by the New York State Assembly to investigate disloyal people, placed Addams' name on the list of subversives.

Jane Addams returned to Europe after World

Despite opposition, Jane Addams continued to participate in peace organizations. After World War I, she was denounced as a communist.

War I and remained very active in the American and international women's peace movements. In 1919 she was elected president of the newly established Women's International League for Peace and Freedom—a position she held until 1929.

In July 1919 Addams discovered 625 German children between the ages of six and thirteen trying to survive on a scant meal a day, sick, hungry, and sometimes dying of malnutrition. When she tried to arouse concern for the children she was accused of having misplaced sympathy for children of enemy soldiers who killed American boys.

When Addams opposed the deportation of aliens on the slimmest of evidence, veterans' organizations denounced her. She seemed woefully out of step with the often bitter and suspicious spirit of the day.

Now in her seventies and in worsening health, Addams returned to Hull House. She sought to help the growing numbers of poor who suffered in the Great Depression. In 1931 Jane Addams was awarded the Nobel Peace Prize, which she shared with American educator Nicholas Murray Butler. The recognition of Addams' accomplishments was overdue. She gave all her prize money to unemployed families at Hull House and to the cause of peace.

Jane Addams, bold crusader for so many causes, died on May 21, 1935. Columnist Walter Lippman wrote: "She had compassion without condescension.

She had pity without retreat into vulgarity. She had infinite sympathy. She was not only good but great."[12] Jane Addams often took her place on the minority side, upholding unpopular causes. She hated war and she became an extremist in her crusade for peace.

Emily Greene Balch

Emily Greene Balch

The Planetary Citizen

On the evening of April 2, 1917, the U.S. Cavalry escorted President Woodrow Wilson toward the Capitol building. He went to stand before an assemblage of dignitaries, including the House of Representatives, the Senate, the Supreme Court, and the Diplomatic Corps. When the President called for a declaration of war, everyone was quickly on their feet—shouting, cheering, and waving aloft hundreds of American flags. As the President returned to the White House, sidewalk crowds continued the cheering. Later, Wilson commented, "My message today was a message of death for our young men. How strange it seems to applaud that." Then, according to his secretary, the President wept.[1] Four days later, on April 6, Emily Greene

Balch sat in the visitors gallery during the roll call in the House of Representatives. She watched as Representative Jeanette Rankin, the first woman to be elected to Congress, cast one of the few votes against U.S. entry into World War I. "I love my country but I cannot vote for war," Rankin said.[2] (Rankin was to be the only person in Congress who would vote against U.S. entry into both World Wars I and II.) Rankin's vote was to be one of Balch's few pleasant moments. In the final tally, the House voted to take the United States to war on the Christian holy day of Good Friday.

Balch noted:

> A war urged by the President on a reluctant Congress upon the grounds of the most disinterested idealism will apparently be "wished upon" the country against its will by the votes of men who fear the press more than they fear their conscience. So, nearly 1,900 years after the death on the Cross, this is to be the celebration of Good Friday.[3]

Emily Balch was born in 1867 in Jamaica Plain, Massachusetts, to a gentle lawyer and his idealistic wife. From the age of nine, the bright young girl kept a diary filled with poems, stories, and commentaries on her life. She would continue this habit of writing in a diary until her death, at age ninety-four.

Balch grew up in a large family, learning the art of reconciliation early. This art was to remain with her throughout her life for, as passionately as she embraced causes, she was never discourteous or rude. Born into a socially and intellectually privileged household, Balch always felt a sense of mission and a duty to service. From her days as a pupil in Miss Ireland's School for girls in Louisburg Square to her years at Bryn Mawr College, she was looking for causes to make the world better.

Early on, as she listened to a minister in her church preach about the evils of war, Balch embraced the cause of pacifism. It fit well with her love for all living things. She had a warm personal affection for all people, and even for plants and animals. But it was her intense interest in different kinds of people that motivated her to study Latin, Greek, Dutch, Russian, Czech, and Polish languages. Balch praised the idea of a "planetary civilization" where everyone worked together. She said, "I am a patriot, and my fatherland is this dear, dear earth."[4]

Balch's interest in immigrants led her to become a specialist in Slavic immigrants and their problems. "We must all work together with them," she said, "for justice, humane conditions of living, for beauty and for true, not merely formal, liberty."[5]

In 1889 Balch used a European fellowship to study economics in Paris. She completed her formal studies at Harvard University and the University of Chicago. Balch then spent a year in Berlin working on economic theories. Upon her return to America she worked at Denison House, helping

Even while a student at Bryn Mawr College, Emily Balch knew her mission was to help others.

poverty-stricken and troubled people—the sort of people she had never met before.

At Denison, Balch worked daily with prisoners, prostitutes, paupers, neglected children, and laborers struggling for decent wages and conditions. It was here that Balch saw a clear cause-and-effect link between economic injustice and crime and war. She decided to teach economics, and at the age of twenty-nine, joined the faculty of Wellesley College in Massachusetts. She also spent time on municipal boards devoted to children's causes.

In addition Balch was involved in women's suffrage and efforts to gain racial justice, amend child labor abuses, and improve working conditions in factories. But the cause most dear to her heart became peace. And to that cause she was about to sacrifice her career.

As a professor at Wellesley, Balch was praised for inspiring her students, who respected the integrity of her fervently held ideals. There was an undercurrent of criticism, however, that her many outside interests sometimes distracted her from her teaching career.

The Spanish-American War of 1898 was enormously popular with the American public and Congress—it lasted less than four months and was a triumph over Spain. Balch, however, opposed it, being one of the very few expressing anti-war sentiments. Then, as growing tensions in Europe led toward World War I, Balch struggled with ideas of how to avoid war. She especially lamented how war divided people and ravaged both crops of the field and cultural heritage.

Balch had a special admiration for the arts, especially the handcrafts of simple people throughout the world. One of her prized personal possessions was a handmade silver necklace given to her by a Slavic peasant. Her links with these people were more strongly forged as she came to admire their spirit. She met Slavic peasants in muddy typhoid-infested neighborhoods in Pennsylvania—where they lived "not in America but underneath America"[6]—as well as in the towns of Europe. War that disrupted the simple lives of the Slavic folk she'd come to love was especially painful.

At first Balch spoke at small peace meetings. Once a man from the American Legion challenged her pacifist views, and she responded with her usual graciousness, defusing his anger. Balch would always maintain the role of apostle of conciliation.

With her close friend, peace activist Jane Addams and other women committed to the cause of peace, Emily Balch began to participate more fully in this cause. She wrote that the new age must be one of fraternal relations among people where equality among classes and nations replaces rivalry. What Balch was proposing was nothing short of revolutionary. She proposed that nationalism—the idea of promoting your own country's welfare over the good of humanity as a whole—should be ended. She also suggested that humankind retain "only that patriotism you can carry into heaven with you."[7]

When World War I broke out, Balch devoted all her efforts to bringing it to a swift conclusion, limiting the suffering and death. This led her to embark on the much ridiculed journey to Europe.

In April of 1915 Emily Balch and forty-one other women sailed for the Netherlands on the Dutch ship *Noordam* to attend the International Congress of Women at the Hague. Undertaking the journey through mined sea lanes and risking confrontation with unfriendly ships required great courage. Balch, Jane Addams, and the others were so devoted to their cause that they ignored these perils.

One morning the ship was detained by British authorities, and newspapers were provided for the ladies to read. In the newspapers Balch and her companions were denounced as pro-German sympathizers, and bitter attacks were made on their characters and goals. When the ship finally docked in the Netherlands, the women joined hundreds of others at the Hague. A center for international peace conferences, the Hague would now see a first in world history—a large group of women meeting to oppose war and to consider ways of preventing it—the International Congress of Women.

Later Balch traveled on the *Oscar II* to Stockholm to attend the Neutral Conference for Continuous Mediation, another gathering that tried to restore peace.

While in Europe, Balch met with women whose

Emily Balch (shown third from left) is pictured with other members of peace groups.

sons and husbands were facing each other on the killing fields of the Western Front. Women from many nations, including the warring countries, had found a common cause. As Balch met in various war capitals to plead for peace, news of her activities reached the trustees of Wellesley College. Newspaper editorials denounced Balch as unpatriotic, and some people felt the economics professor had become a liability to the school. The trustees, who first considered not renewing Balch's contract in 1918, met to consider her future. Balch had taught at Wellesley, serving not only as professor but as department head in both the economics and sociology disciplines, for twenty years.

While she attended a peace conference in May 1919, Balch was informed that she would not be reappointed to the faculty. Her prolonged absences from teaching were cited as contributing factors, but the basic reason for her dismissal was that she'd become too controversial. This was borne out when a January 24, 1919, military intelligence report identified Emily Balch on a list of pro-German pacifists—an ominous distinction!

Emily Balch was now fifty-two years old and out of work. Unemployment was not an appealing prospect for a woman far from being independently wealthy. With characteristic good will, however, Balch described herself as shocked but not embittered by the dismissal. She said she understood the predicament of the trustees at Wellesley.

After leaving Wellesley, Balch helped establish the Women's International League for Peace and Freedom, serving as its first secretary-treasurer. She continued to work for this and other peace groups as well as writing articles and promoting the development of the League of Nations. In the years between World Wars I and II, Balch could usually be seen dressed in drab blues and grays, blending with the ordinary people she worked with at the settlement houses.

When World War II came, Balch was confronted with a painful moral decision. She wrestled with her pacifist conscience. This situation was unlike that of World War I, when nationalistic ambitions clashed but neither side displayed profound evil. This time the monstrous figure of Adolf Hitler was on the world scene. Like all decent people, Balch shared the horror and grief over the persecution of Jews by Hitler. Yet how could she abandon her lifelong commitment to nonviolent resolutions of all problems?

Balch finally broke ranks with some of her pacifist friends to support American participation in World War II. In opposition to her beloved Women's International League for Peace and Freedom, she decided that war was preferable to a world dominated by Hitler.

In spite of her support for the war effort, Balch courageously opposed the rounding up and detention of thousands of Japanese Americans on the west coast. She was one of the very few Americans who stood against the internment of Japanese Americans, who were thought to be security risks. The majority of Americans took nearly half a century to agree with her position.

After World War II, Balch became a strong supporter of the United Nations (UN). She feared the growing rivalry between the communist world and the free nations of the West. She also was an enthusiastic supporter of American efforts to rebuild war torn Europe.

In 1946 Emily Balch was awarded the Nobel Peace Prize for her lifelong devotion to the cause of peace. In her Nobel Prize address, Balch expressed the hope that a new European epoch would bring Europe to the fore as a "mother of culture" and no longer a "mother of wars."[8] She donated her prize money to the peace groups she'd always worked with. In tribute to her it was said that her accomplishments were all the more praiseworthy because of her unique ability to sway minds with reason.

Emily Balch spent her last years tending her African violets and occasionally visiting friends. In spite of the continuing world tensions of the Cold War, she had confidence in the spirit of humankind and she remained optimistic about the chances for permanent peace. A little past her ninety-fourth birthday, Balch passed from the planet earth, loving everyone and everything, cheerful to the end.

Mairead Corrigan and Betty Williams

Mairead Corrigan and Betty Williams

Guerrillas for Peace

On August 11, 1976, a young Irish mother named Anne Maguire decided to take a chance and go out into the streets of Belfast, Northern Ireland, with her three small children. There had been serious violence in Belfast, but surely a mother and her innocent children wouldn't be fair game for the warring factions. So Maguire began her fateful stroll with eight-year-old Joanne, two-and-one-half-year-old John, and six-week-old Andrew.

Before the family had gone very far the sounds of gunfire crackled off the sides of buildings along the sidewalk. Everything happened then with horrifying speed.

Minutes earlier a carload of men from the Irish Republican Army (IRA), a Catholic paramilitary group, screamed to a brief stop alongside a group of British soldiers. The IRA men peppered the British soldiers with gunfire and then sped off in their car. Several soldiers ran to their cars to take chase after the IRA gunmen. A gunfire-punctuated car chase was now underway through the streets of Belfast.

The driver of the IRA getaway car, a young man named Danny Lennon, was shot through the head by a British trooper. Lennon died instantly at the wheel, causing the car to plunge onto the sidewalk. At this point the car careened into the stunned Maguire family.

Mairead Corrigan, Anne Maguire's sister, was summoned to the hospital in Belfast by a grief-stricken brother-in-law, Jackie Maguire. He said, "My three children are dead. My darling Anne is dying. Oh, how will I live without my darling Anne and my children?"[1] Mairead Corrigan viewed the bodies of the three little children lying side by side in the hospital. Their crushed bodies resembled the pitiful remains of all war victims. But this tragedy had happened on a neighborhood street where families shopped and children played.

Anne Maguire recovered from her physical wounds, but she never fully recovered from the shock of losing her children. Four years later, hopelessly trapped in depression, she took her own life.

And so the tragedy on that quiet Belfast street claimed its fourth victim.

Mairead Corrigan, like all who lived in Northern Ireland, was well aware of the region's violent past. Ireland, predominantly a Catholic country, had been fighting British rule for centuries. Finally Great Britain yielded to the Irish struggle for independence. But the Protestant Irish demanded that they not be forced to live in a unified independent Ireland under Catholic majority rule.

After much hesitation, Great Britain reached a compromise. In 1922 the northern part of Ireland, where Protestants were in the majority, was allowed to remain under British rule, while the southern part of the country, where Catholics were in the majority, was allowed to become independent. About one third of the people in Northern Ireland were Catholic, and these people would have preferred to join the Catholic south in independence.

The Protestants in Northern Ireland had more power and access to better jobs than the Catholic minority, who was discriminated against. Catholic frustrations grew, and outbreaks of violence marked the 1920s and 1930s. Then, inspired by the success of the civil rights movement in the United States, Irish Catholics of Northern Ireland grew more adamant in their demands for equality. There were street marches and riots.

In 1968 Catholics scheduled a peaceful protest march, but the Protestant government forbade it.

The marchers took to the streets anyway, and the protest degenerated into rock throwing and vandalism. Great Britain sent troops to Northern Ireland in order to protect the Catholic population against excesses from the Protestant majority, but soon Catholics felt that the British soldiers were merely allies of the Protestant power structure.

Bombings became a tool of the increasingly bitter conflict. In 1971, in only four months, eight hundred violent incidents in Northern Ireland claimed the lives of thirty-one soldiers and seventy-one civilians. By the time Anne Maguire ventured into that Belfast street in 1976, sixteen hundred civilians had died.

Thirty-five-year-old Betty Williams, a Catholic mother of two and occasional waitress, had been at the scene of the accident when the Maguires were struck. That evening while watching television, she heard a sobbing Mairead Corrigan say, "It's not violence that people want. Only one percent of the people of this province want this slaughter."[2] Williams began at once to circulate petitions against the violence, and in forty-eight hours she had six thousand signatures. "We must rid the community of this riffraff," she said of the violent men. "That's all they are—bums!"[3]

Corrigan heard of Williams' efforts and invited her to the Maguire children's funeral. From that meeting arose the friendship of the two women and the peace movement they started. There had never before been a peace movement in Northern Ireland. There seemed to be too much bitterness and fear to permit Catholics and Protestants to form a united front for peace.

Neither Corrigan nor Williams had the least experience in organization. They decided to learn by doing and to simply follow their hearts. Though they were very different in natures, they worked well together.

Mairead Corrigan was born January 27, 1944, in the Catholic ghetto of Falls, West Belfast. She was one of seven children and attended Catholic schools until, at age sixteen, she went to work as a bookkeeper. Twice, while defending friends against what she considered indecent searches, Corrigan was beaten by British soldiers. She was deeply religious and a pacifist by nature. Still single in her early thirties, Corrigan lived at home with her parents.

Betty Williams was born in 1941 in Belfast and married a Protestant engineer in the merchant marine. Outgoing and forceful, she frequently lost her waitress jobs for her strong convictions. Williams was generally pro-IRA until one day when she saw a young British soldier shot. He fell almost at her feet, and she knelt beside the dying boy and prayed with him. She was severely criticized by some of her Catholic neighbors for showing compassion to one of the "enemy." This incident caused Williams to rethink her politics, and she began to see both sides as human beings.

A tall handsome woman, Williams sometimes admits to a hot temper and has said, "I'm not like Mairead. People who know Mairead and me call us the saint and the sinner!"[4]

These two unlikely crusaders began with a small movement of fifty women marching together to protest the activities of paramilitary groups such as the IRA. The original fifty were all Catholic, but Protestant women who yearned for peace were also invited to join and they soon did. To suggest that Catholics and Protestants might march together in Northern Ireland for any reason was seen by many as madness.

However, the small band of women marched through Belfast, the capital of Northern Ireland, keeping to the Catholic neighborhoods. Gradually their ranks swelled as women, young and old, streamed from houses and stores to fall in line behind the peace banners. They sang non-sectarian hymns (neither specifically Catholic nor Protestant) and recited non-sectarian prayers so Protestants might feel comfortable in participating.

Finally there were about ten thousand women marching in the name of peace. But the onlookers were not all peaceful. Many looked upon the marchers as traitors to the Catholic cause. Among those watching were a growing band of militants who tossed eggs and even bricks at Corrigan and Williams. At one rally Williams, in a red sweater and red pants, was singing "When Irish Eyes Are Smiling" in her gravelly voice when the hecklers almost drowned her out. She sang louder and then yelled, "Look at them! They're not Irishmen! They don't even know what they are!"[5]

The peace movement distributed a booklet, "The Price of Peace," and became known as the "Peace People."[6] The IRA said of them, "The peace movement wants peace at any price. It is nothing more than a facade for a British government operation."[7] On the other side, well-known Protestant partisan Ian Paisley said the peace movement was bad because "it refuses to support the military defeat of the IRA."[8] A bitterly partisan Protestant newspaper said, "The more IRA coffins, the fewer innocent people will suffer, and if need be, we will have to step on the toes of the members of the peace movement who stand between the enemy and the army."[9]

Corrigan, Williams, and their friends, however, refused to be intimidated by fists, rocks, or violent words. A little bloodied, but more determined than ever, they planned a march through a Protestant neighborhood. Thirty-five thousand Catholic and Protestant volunteers came together to plan such future marches.

Twenty thousand marched through Londonderry, the most bitterly segregated of all the towns in Northern Ireland. Until the march, Catholics dared not set foot in Protestant territory in Londonderry and vice versa. But now, arms linked, praying and singing together, women of both religions boldly marched forward.

The organization, now formally called Peace People, wrote a constitution in which they outlined not only projects to ease the tensions between Protestants and Catholics, but also social programs to lessen the frustration in the neighborhoods. Now they would not only march, but also provide meals on wheels to the aged, help for overworked mothers, and social activities for children and youth too long scarred by violence.[10]

Williams decided to debate her opinions with some IRA women in her home. Twenty minutes later she lay beaten on the floor of her own house, convincing even the fiery Williams that much more needed to be done in the way of reconciliation.

By March 1977 the Peace People had more than three hundred thousand signatures on its Declaration of Peace. Both Corrigan and Williams visited the United States to generally enthusiastic receptions. They were pleading with Americans, especially American-Irish Catholics, to stop sending money to para-military groups such as the IRA, who used the money to make bombs and buy guns.

Irish businesses were encouraged to move into economically depressed neighborhoods to provide jobs, especially to people in riot-torn areas. A major source of Catholic unrest centered on the high jobless rate. If employment went up, tensions would go down. One success story involved a woman opening a stationery, plant, and leather goods store where no other business had ever been brave enough to venture. However, so much more needed to be done.

By October 1976 a Nobel Peace Prize had not yet been given for that year. During this month the surprise announcement came that the Nobel Prize Committee was awarding the 1976 Nobel Prize to Mairead Corrigan and Betty Williams. Hearing the news Corrigan wept and said, "To me, the Nobel Peace Prize means that we can change the world through nonviolence, and many people will keep that vision before them as I will."[11]

In the Nobel Prize ceremony the committee described the women as "guerrillas for peace," who "by their initiative encouraged a great movement of aversion to violence in Ulster."[12]

After receiving the Nobel Peace Prize, Corrigan and Williams continued their work for a nonviolent solution to the problems of Northern Ireland. Now married, Mairead Corrigan Maguire addressed the Pax Christi USA National Assembly in 1990 with these words:

> There is nothing like the smile of a newborn baby to bring out the best in each of us. My mother always says that when a baby first smiles, it is because the baby sees the angels. We know the child needs to live in an atmosphere of peace in its own home. Peace in its community. Peace in its wider home, planet Earth.[13]

Mairead Corrigan Maguire admitted that Northern

Mairead Corrigan and Betty Williams continue their involvement in
Northern Ireland's peace movement. Here, Corrigan is shown at the
1992 Pax Christi Assembly.

Ireland continues to be a victim of violence. So many years after the peace movement began, fear and hatred still cause bombs to detonate and the innocent to die. But there has been an increase in groups working for peace. Maguire said that so many groups have now organized that it's difficult to keep track of them all.

"What is needed in the world today is the unambiguous proclamation that violence is a lie," Maguire said. Confiding that when she asked Mother Teresa for advice in how to persevere in the struggle, Mother Teresa said, "Oh, pray, pray all the time."[14]

In Northern Ireland brutal violence still continues. But the work of these two women and their hundreds of thousands of friends continues as well. There is hope that the candles they light will eventually snuff out the darkness of hatred, fear, and injustice in their troubled homeland.

Mother Teresa

Mother Teresa
Saint of the Gutter

One day in 1949 a man lay dying on the roadside in Calcutta, India. A small dark-skinned woman found him and asked personnel in an adjacent hospital if he couldn't be brought in for care. Her request was refused, so she went to a chemist to get medicine. By the time she returned to the man's side, he had died. The woman—Mother Teresa—did not hide her feelings at such a tragedy. "They look after a dog or cat better than a fellow man," she said.[1] Caring for such abandoned and unloved people has become the ministry of Mother Teresa. Her increasingly bent figure and her craggy lined face have become familiar to the poor and dying all over the world.

The remarkable story of Mother Teresa began on

August 27, 1910, in the small Macedonian (Yugo-slavian) town of Skopje. Her name was Gonxha (Agnes) Bojaxhiu and she was an Albanian. Her father, a successful building contractor, was an Albanian nationalist, and with many others, he hoped to see his country independent again. One night, when Gonxha was just nine years old, her father returned from a political meeting very ill and hemorrhaging. He died quickly and some in the family believed he had been poisoned by his political enemies.

Gonxha's mother was left to support her family of three children with a business in embroidered handcrafts and she did so very well. Young Gonxha loved music and had a lovely singing voice, which she used in the choir. Friends described her as a lively, pretty, mischievous child who always seemed full of joy. But Gonxha had a serious side as well, as her mother's strong religious faith had a major impact on her.

Once a woman in Skopje was so sick and with-out money that she couldn't even get help from her family. There was no one to care for her so Gonxha's mother took her into her own home and looked after her until she was well. Gonxha was impressed by such charity and she always carried the memory of her mother's extraordinary act of kindness.[2]

When Gonxha was a schoolgirl, a priest showed her and her classmates a large map of the world. He marked all the places where missions served the poor. Gonxha studied the map with great interest. Then she amazed the class by explaining in detail all the good works going on in those faraway places. The priest was also impressed with the girl's knowledge and he mentioned to her that his religious order was related to the Sisters of Loreto. This group of religious women was devoted to the education of young girls around the world.

When Gonxha announced her intention to become a nun, her brother Lazar was surprised. He thought life in the convent would be too dull and quiet for his vivacious sister. "A girl like *you?*" he questioned in disbelief, "became a nun?"[3] Teenaged Gonxha replied that Lazar, a soldier, felt important serving a king who ruled two million subjects. She said she would be serving the king of the world— God.

On November 29, 1928, Gonxha Bojaxhui arrived in Dublin, Ireland, where the Sisters of Loreto had sent her to learn English. Gonxha needed to master this language before she could be sent to India to teach in English. Shy and small, the young Albanian could not speak a word of English. Adapting to a whole new world proved to be quite an adjustment, but in three years she was ready to take up her work.

At the age of twenty-one, Sister Teresa (she had chosen the religious name Teresa) began teaching history and geography at St. Mary's School for girls located in Entally, a district of Calcutta. Her students were the daughters of the wealthy. In fact, the sisters did not come in contact with the desperately poor areas of Calcutta. Sometimes, though, Sister Teresa looked beyond the huge walls of St. Mary's—down into the slums of Moti Jheel where families huddled together in stark poverty. She saw beggars and lepers who lived and died in the streets in the midst of textile and chemical factories, and these people began to haunt her. Sister Teresa tried at first to combine some outreach to the poor with her teaching career. But on September 10, 1946, while traveling by train she said she heard a call from God. The message was to "give up all and follow Christ into the slums to serve Him among the poorest of the poor."[4]

Sister Teresa got permission from the Catholic Church to found a new religious order, the Missionaries of Charity. The order's purpose would be to offer "wholehearted free service to the poorest of the poor, of all castes and creeds."[5] The women of the order would dress in traditional Indian clothes— white saris with blue borders. They would live simple austere lives among the poor, and their philosophy would be "no one has a right to a superfluity of wealth while others are dying of starvation."[6]

Sister Teresa was now the head of her order, becoming "Mother Teresa," at the age of thirty-six. She would have as her personal possessions only a small bed, a wooden table to write on, and a bucket for washing her sari. She explained "Before God, we are all poor."[7]

Mother Teresa began her work renting a private garden between hovels (shacks) in the slums of Matizhil for five rupees (about twenty cents) a month. Here Mother Teresa taught the poor children of the streets, most of whom had never before been inside a school. She firmly believed that the advantage of education belongs to all, not just the wealthy. The school was makeshift, without tables, desks, or chalkboards. Mother Teresa would smooth a spot on the dirt and write words and math problems with a sharpened stick. She taught reading, writing, and even such basic tasks as how to use a bar of soap for washing. Most of the children had never before held a bar of soap in their hands.

When Mother Teresa finished her day's work teaching her thirty students, she often went to visit the sick and search for abandoned babies and orphan children on rubbish heaps. Eventually she became a roving clinic, carrying medicines and food to the poor on the streets.

In 1949 generous individuals began sending help, and a two-storied building at 14 Creek Lane in Calcutta was donated to Mother Teresa. Soon she accepted her first recruit, a Bengali girl who took the name of Agnes in honor of Mother Teresa. More dedicated young women followed. Twenty-six sisters joined, followed by young men who became brothers

(Catholic men who take vows of poverty and chastity but are not priests).

In 1952 Mother Teresa found a dying woman who had been half eaten by rats and ants. She carried her from the place, trying to find a hospital, but no facility would take in the woman. Mother Teresa cared for her, then decided that the Missionaries of Charity must open a home for the dying because there was no place for suffering people such as this woman.

Mother Teresa and her sisters found a Hindu temple originally built in 1809. The temple served as a way station for pilgrims offering devotion to Kali, a Hindu deity. The devotions had fallen off over the years, and now the temple was abandoned except for a few Hindu monks who stayed there. Mother Teresa moved in with her sick charges, causing one of the Hindu monks to object to this high-handed action. Other monks sided with Mother Teresa. One man said that Mother Teresa and her patients would not be ordered from the building "before you get your mothers and sisters to do the work these nuns are doing."[8] This view prevailed, and now Mother Teresa had her home for the dying. Of the people she rescued from death in the streets she said, "They lived like animals. At least they die like human beings."[9]

In 1957 Mother Teresa's work expanded to include people suffering from leprosy (an infectious disease that causes deformities). She built "Shantinagar," or the City of Peace. Leprosy could now be cured with modern drugs, but since many lepers were already deformed, they became outcasts without jobs and were forced to beg for their daily food. At the City of Peace, the patients received medicine to keep their disease under control and they also learned a trade. Later Mother Teresa built a community for lepers unable to find any other shelter.

Mother Teresa helped other communities offering care. Shishu Bhavan was built to house destitute and ill children, and Prem Dan was a large compound for mentally and physically handicapped people. When asked how she manages to cope with all her work, Mother Teresa said, "It's simple. I pray."[10]

In all her work among the suffering, Mother Teresa always insisted that the medicine and care given was not as important as the love. "The poor must know that we love them, that they are wanted," she said.[11]

Her concern extends even to the unborn, as she has taken a strong pro-life viewpoint. "Please don't destroy the child," she said, "we will take the child."[12] To help with population control in India, Mother Teresa and her sisters teach natural family planning, which has sharply reduced the number of unplanned pregnancies.

Mother Teresa's work spread to all corners of the world, including more than twenty-five countries. Her legacy includes orphanages, schools, free clinics, and leprosariums. In 1971 the sisters went to the South Bronx, New York, and set up a system whereby hot meals are brought to the elderly and homebound. The sisters also offer services in St. Louis, Detroit, and San Diego.

Stories and legends about Mother Teresa abound. For instance, it is said that once a pouring rain fell on ninety-five cartons of precious powdered milk in an Indian courtyard. However, the milk destined for Mother Teresa's poor was dry and undamaged. When Mother Teresa needed to fly to one of her missions but lacked the money for a ticket, she offered to serve as a flight attendant for her fare. Instead the airline gave her a lifetime free pass.

In 1979 Mother Teresa was chosen to receive the Nobel Peace Prize. Professor John Sanness, Chairman of the Nobel Prize Committee in Oslo said:

> She had a glimpse of the poverty and squalor of the slums, of sick people who remained untended, of lonely men and women lying down to die on the pavement, of the thousands of orphaned children wandering around with no one to care for them. It was among these people that she felt a call to work, and to spend the rest of her life. . . .[13]

Mother Teresa saw the Nobel Prize not as a tribute to her, but as a recognition of the existence of

Mother Teresa was chosen to receive the Nobel Peace Prize in 1979. She saw the prize as a recognition of the existence of the poor in the world and the importance of helping them.

the poor in the world and the importance of helping
them. In her Nobel Prize address she noted:

> We don't need bombs and guns to destroy,
> to bring peace—just get together, love one
> another, bring that peace, that joy, that
> strength of presence of each other in the
> home. And we will be able to overcome all
> the evil that is in the world. There is so much
> suffering, so much hatred, so much misery,
> and we with our prayer, with our sacrifice are
> beginning at home. Love begins at home,
> and it is not how much we do, but how
> much love we put into the action that we
> do.[14]

Since receiving the Nobel Peace Prize, Mother
Teresa has continued her energetic service to the
poor. From Calcutta to Bangladesh, from Addis
Ababa to Harlem, she has visited the sick and the
homeless, the poor in health, and the lonely in spirit.
Mother Teresa has received many other honors in
addition to the Nobel Peace Prize, including honor-
ary doctorates from great universities. She has also
earned the admiration of famous people such as U.S.
Presidents Jimmy Carter and Ronald Reagan, and
India's Indira Gandhi—all who praised her work.
One of the most powerful tributes appeared in a
newspaper editorial which said in part:

> Most of the recipients of the Nobel Peace
> Prize over the years have been politicians or
> diplomats. But Mother Teresa, the nun who
> founded the Missionaries of Charity, has

spent the last thirty-one years working with the destitute and dying in the slums of Calcutta. It is the example of personal devotion to these people, as individuals, that is compelling. The award is, among other things, a reminder of a kind of poverty that most Europeans and Americans are unlikely ever to see. Occasionally the Norwegian Nobel Committee uses the prize to remind the world that there is more than one kind of peace and that politics is not the only way to pursue it.[15]

Of all the tributes showered upon this humble woman of peace, probably none are as poignant as the many letters and drawings she receives from children all over the world. Even the youngest children seem to understand the importance of her work. As Mother Teresa related:

Some time ago in Calcutta we had great difficulty getting sugar, and I don't know how the word got around to the children, and a little boy of four years old, Hindu boy, went home and told his parents: I will not eat sugar for three days, I will give my sugar to Mother Teresa for her children. After three days his father and mother brought him to our house. I had never met them before, and this little one could scarcely pronounce my name, but he knew exactly what he had come to do. He knew that he wanted to share his love.[16]

Alva Myrdal

Alva Myrdal

Conscience of Disarmament

In October 1962 U.S. President John F. Kennedy was confronting a possible nuclear war. Soviet missiles had been placed less than one hundred miles from the American mainland in Cuba.

Kennedy pondered the dreadful prospect of possible death for all the innocent children of the world who would never have a chance if this was indeed the beginning of the third, and perhaps the final, world war. Armageddon loomed as a real possibility—the end of life on earth as nuclear weapons rained death upon the planet.

Appearing before the American people on television, October 22, 1962, President Kennedy said, "We will not prematurely or unnecessarily risk the costs of worldwide nuclear war in which even the fruits of victory would be ashes in our mouth, but neither will we shrink from that risk at any time it must be faced."[1]

Alva Myrdal, a sixty-year-old Swedish diplomat listened to Kennedy's speech with the rest of the world, only she had more knowledge of what nuclear war meant than most people. Myrdal had devoted much of her adult life to trying to solve the terrible problem of nuclear armaments piling up around the world. She had said that in the atomic age we could no longer depend on the next generation arriving as surely as the seasons. And now, in Kennedy's speech, Myrdal and the world experienced the dread that their worst nightmare might be at hand.

The world found a peaceful way around the Cuban Missile Crisis, and Myrdal continued to work for peace with an even greater sense of urgency. Of all her many interests in life, this would be her greatest passion.

Alva Reimer was born in 1902 in Uppsala, Sweden, and it was soon apparent to her parents that this was no ordinary little girl. Her family farmed, and Alva's father saw agriculture as the most important work anybody could do. The farmer was involved in bringing forth food for humanity. Alva's parents wanted all their children to share in such chores as milking the cows and bringing in the hay. But Alva had plans far beyond farm life. She talked about "fantastic"[2] plans for her future.

Alva dreamed of someday escaping the stifling rural environment and finding her inner talents. The little farm girl was convinced that she'd grow to be an exciting and interesting woman who would make a difference in the world.

In elementary school Alva was a good student. She loved to play outdoors, and while her female classmates were engaged in gentler pursuits, she was wildly playing with the boys. Alva also wrote poems as a child, inventing a dramatic poem about the brave Vikings when she was twelve.

Alva's father believed that the seven years of school customarily given to girls was plenty for his daughter. So, at the age of fifteen, Alva Reimer was expected to be finished with her education. But how could she achieve her "fantastic" plans with only an elementary school education?

Instead of remaining on the farm and socializing with neighboring farm boys as her friends were doing, Reimer took a job in town helping people with their tax returns. With her small salary she helped her family, bought books, and saved for her future education.

At the age of seventeen, Reimer found a college that would accept her, the University of Stockholm. Though she had no secondary school background she could gain a college degree if she kept up with the university work. Reimer worked hard in college while continuing to earn a salary to pay her tuition. She was eventually awarded a college degree from the University of Stockholm in June 1922, at the age of twenty. Reimer was already in love. At seventeen she'd met a lanky twenty-year-old university student named Gunnar Myrdal. Myrdal shared Reimer's dreams of doing something important in the world. Like her, he was not content to spend his life in quiet pursuits in Sweden. Both possessing strong personalities and great ambition, Reimer and Myrdal bounced their ideas off one another. They were kindred spirits, and in October 1924, they were married. Three children were born to the Myrdals—Sissela, Jan, and Kaj.

Alva Myrdal had so many ideas about improving so many things that it was difficult to know what project she ought to tackle first. She was especially interested in the subject of child rearing and school reform. One of her pet projects was to make sure other young girls wouldn't be faced, as she had been, with limited opportunities for further education.

In 1929 the Myrdals traveled to the United States to pursue their interests in a more stimulating environment. They arrived just before the stock market crashed, and soon saw the devastation of economic decline on the lives of ordinary people. While Gunnar Myrdal worked in the field of economics, Alva Myrdal studied ways of enabling poor children to develop their full potential. Sometimes their two fields of interest merged. This occurred when Alva Myrdal urged full equality for everyone as the answer to many of society's problems while Gunnar

Myrdal demonstrated how inequality harmed African Americans in his landmark work, *An American Dilemma.*

Alva Myrdal urged equality not only among classes, but between men and women, and even between children and adults. During these years she was devoting a lot of time to her three small children, and she took special delight in their developing potential. Though tone deaf, Myrdal sang her children to sleep at bedtime. She also shared word games, fairy tales, and the accounts of explorers with them. Myrdal was a masterful storyteller—a skill honed in rural Sweden where, on long cold nights, the skilled storyteller was invaluable. Myrdal strove to give her own children that sense of equality with their parents that she wanted for all children.

In the years just before World War II, the Myrdals were busy working and raising their children. But the descending hostilities cast a pall over them. Outspoken anti-Fascists, the Myrdals faced a dilemma—should they return to Sweden and share the fate of their countrymen? Hitler had already conquered Norway despite a brave resistance, and Denmark was also invaded by the Nazi army. Could Sweden be any luckier than the other Scandinavian countries? The Myrdals decided to return to Sweden to take their chances.

In 1943, when it was clear that the Allies were winning and Hitler would likely be defeated, Alva Myrdal devoted her energies to writing against anti-Semitism and fighting persecution of the disabled. As Gunnar Myrdal was publishing *An American Dilemma,* Alva Myrdal was turning toward the career that would dominate the rest of her life—diplomacy.

In 1949 Alva Myrdal accepted the position as head of the United Nations (UN) Department of Social Welfare, tackling problems of women, children, housing, and education. She worked to remove obstacles posed by the war and the flood of refugees in postwar Europe. Some displaced persons fled the ravages of war, and many more were now escaping from countries that had come under communist domination. In her new job Myrdal lamented, "It is hard to imagine the depths and breadth of the black misery besetting this world. It seems incredible that more than one half of this world's inhabitants go hungry today."[3]

Later Myrdal moved to Paris to head UNESCO's Department of Social Sciences. UNESCO stands for United Nations Educational, Scientific and Cultural organization, which seeks to promote friendship and cooperation among nations by shared work in education, science, and culture. Myrdal's formidable task was to revive the scientific institutes and universities destroyed by the war and to introduce these institutions in new and developing countries. Myrdal forcefully fought the idea that there were higher and lower races, insisting that all humans—regardless of race—were capable of great

As director of the UN Department of Social Welfare, Alva Myrdal continued to improve the lives of many who struggled for survival in postwar Europe. Here she is shown with Assistant Secretary-General for Social Affairs Henri Lougier.

achievement. Myrdal's work in UNESCO was widely praised.[4]

In 1955 Alva Myrdal became Swedish Ambassador to India, Burma (now called Myanmar), and Ceylon (now called Sri Lanka). She found India's widespread poverty sad, but the people impressed her with their philosophy of life. They were not striving for material items as much as the people in the West. She also found much to admire in their harmony with their environment. As she traveled through these countries, she was a great success in spreading good will.

Gunnar Myrdal worked on the UN Economic Commission for Europe while Alva Myrdal began to work on disarmament proposals that Sweden would present to the United Nations. Because of their busy schedules, they were often apart. As fears of nuclear war grew with the Cold War, Alva Myrdal redoubled her efforts to spread the cause of disarmament. She immersed herself in the study of nuclear weapons and how they might be controlled, lest human life be doomed.

Elected to the Senate of the *Riksdag* in 1961, Myrdal now worked as a member of the Swedish parliament to promote her idea of a "non-Atom club,"[5] which stressed the role of non-nuclear nations in contributing to the disarmament debate. Since all nations are vulnerable to nuclear war, she argued, all should have a voice in how to solve the problem. She felt that nations such as Sweden, which were free of nuclear arms, must set an example by promising not to produce or harbor the weapons.

Alva Myrdal was never a total pacifist—she saw lasting peace as a distant goal and wanted only to limit the role of war and reduce the nuclear threat. She had supported Finland's efforts to repel Soviet aggression in 1939–1940, and she supported the Allies against Hitler. She even allowed for the need for some military deterrence, admitting that the idea of nuclear innocence was hopeless.

In January 1964 Secretary-General U Thant appointed Myrdal to an expert committee to study the problems of apartheid (a system of racial separation) in South Africa.[6] And in 1966 she was a member of an eighteen-nation committee on disarmament meeting in Geneva. But her most significant contribution to peace was the founding of the Stockholm International Peace Research Institute in 1965.

In 1975 Alva Myrdal began work on *The Game of Disarmament*, a substantial work that chided the super powers for trying to avoid disarmament.[7] Gunnar Myrdal had won the Nobel Prize for Economics the previous year. By now both Myrdals were feeling the weight of their years. Alva Myrdal was also coping with illness, but she pressed on—convinced of the vital nature of her work. She believed in always pressing on to accomplish something if you could.

In the early 1980s, as President Ronald Reagan

took office in the United States with his fiery rhetoric describing the Soviet Union as the "evil empire," the struggle for meaningful disarmament seemed more urgent than ever. Alva Myrdal ignored her weariness and declining health to work more diligently toward world peace. For these efforts she received the first Albert Einstein Peace Prize given to honor "the person who has contributed most significantly to the prevention of nuclear war and to the strengthening of international peace."

In October 1982 Alva Myrdal was chosen to win the Nobel Peace Prize. She was honored for work toward peace carried on in spite of great reason for pessimism. She had campaigned against aggressive rhetoric from world leaders, decried the militarization of world civilization, and denounced the rising tide of terrorism.

Myrdal was now eighty years old and she seemed like a woman who had achieved it all. She had spent her life doing challenging and important work while devoting much love and energy to the rearing of the three Myrdal children. Her husband, Gunnar, was still at her side, supporting but not overshadowing her. Numerous times Alva Myrdal had been called Sweden's most admired woman. Just as she dreamed it would be, her life was filled with campaigns for important causes.

In February 1986, one day after her eighty-fourth birthday, Alva Myrdal died. During the church service the Bishop of Stockholm said that she had inspired many people and she left as her monument a bright faith in the future.

Throughout her long life Alva Myrdal was described in many ways, but perhaps none fit her so well as when she was called "the conscience of the disarmament movement." Alva Myrdal's devoted husband followed her in death a little more than one year later.

Daw Aung San Suu Kyi

7

Daw Aung San Suu Kyi
Heroine of the "Golden Land"

In the fall of 1988, excitement was in the air as thousands of people neared the capital of Rangoon, Burma (now called Yangon, Myanmar). Then, suddenly, army trucks disgorged armed soldiers, and machine gun fire poured from the rooftops along the street. Many of the demonstrators were shot and others were crushed to death beneath the wheels of the trucks. "It was a slaughter," reported Burmese journalist U Win Khet. "I saw children lying dead. One little girl in her school uniform was still clutching a flag, sprawled in a pool of blood."[1] The people of Burma were crying out for democracy, and marching at their head was a slim woman named Daw Aung San Suu Kyi (pronounced dah ông san soo chē).

Suu Kyi was born in Burma in 1945, the daughter of General Aung San, leader of Burma's independence movement. When the Japanese invaded British-controlled Burma in 1942, General Aung San fought the Japanese invaders, and once they were driven out, he opposed continued British occupation. He wanted to free Burma from *all* foreign control. Suu Kyi was just two years old in 1947 when her father was assassinated.

Burma received its independence from the British Commonwealth in 1948, but the nation was still not free from troubles. In 1962 Burma's shaky democracy was overthrown by General Ne Win, who established a regime that was a form of military socialism. The eccentric Ne Win ended freedom of the press, banned political parties, and severely damaged the economy of his country—once called the "Golden Land" for its flourishing trade. Ne Win's army, the *Tatmadaw*, ruled with an iron hand.

At the age of fifteen, Suu Kyi moved to India, and later, to England where she received a degree from Oxford University. She was married to British scholar Michael Aris, and two sons—Alexander and Kim—were born to the couple. Though Suu Kyi lived abroad, her homeland remained in her heart. In 1988 Suu Kyi returned to Burma, after a twenty-eight-year absence, to be with her ailing mother.

In July 1988 Ne Win had officially retired, but the Tatmadaw swiftly created the State Law-and-Order Restoration Council, renaming the country

Myanmar in 1989 and then renaming the capital Yangon. Renaming both the country and the capital were efforts to show a distinct break with the past and the beginning of a military socialistic regime.

Suu Kyi found her country in terrible shape. Freedom didn't exist, and the economy was in shambles. Once the richest country in southeast Asia with an abundance of agricultural products (rice, grain, sorghums, and oil seeds) and a booming export business, Burma was now granted "least developed nation" status by the United Nations in 1987. The annual inflation rate soared to between thirty and forty percent. And the once beautiful streets, legendary in the world, crumbled into potholed nightmares with backed-up sewage. The per capita income in 1990 declined to $318 a year, one of the lowest in the world.

Demonstrations demanding a return to democracy were already underway in the country when Suu Kyi used her charismatic speaking skills to join in the struggle. "I could not, as my father's daughter, remain indifferent," she told the half million people who came to hear her speak in Rangoon. "This is our second struggle for independence."[2]

Severe repression followed the protests by students, merchants, monks, homemakers, and even children. The Tatmadaw set up ambushes and shot fleeing students in the back. Female students were raped, and forty-one arrested students suffocated while locked in a police van.

Between one and three thousand people were killed during the uprising. When nurses protested by carrying banners that pleaded with the army to stop firing on the crowds, they too were shot. Bodies were piled before the public crematorium. Witnesses alleged that the wounded who were still alive were hurled into the ovens along with the dead.[3]

The government promised free elections in 1990, but few believed they would happen. Suu Kyi helped found the National League for Democracy (NLD) to take part in elections should they occur. Meanwhile those arrested were taken before military tribunals (which, in reality, were just sentencing forums). If a person was arrested, his or her guilt was assumed. Some students were beaten and released as a warning to others. It became illegal even to publicly express sorrow for fallen friends.

Suu Kyi charged the government with violations of civil rights and with lying about having free elections. She said that General U Ne Win still held control of the country from behind the scenes. In spite of the dire consequences of speaking out against the government, she continued to defy military rulers.

On July 20, 1988, the government charged Suu Kyi and her party deputy with posing a threat to the armed forces and promoting anarchy. Suu Kyi was placed under house arrest in the capital of Rangoon. House arrest keeps people confined to their home as prisoners are confined to jail. Every day soldiers took

At a rally in Rangoon, Burma, Aung San Suu Kyi addresses an audience gathered to demand democracy.

their places in four sentry boxes in front of the compound where Suu Kyi lived.

When elections were finally held in 1990, Suu Kyi was still under tight house arrest and unable to campaign for her party candidates. In spite of this handicap, the NLD won 80 percent of the seats in the proposed National Assembly, gaining 392 out of 485 assembly places. Despite this amazing election triump, the military government, now led by General Saw Maung, remained firmly in power. It was as if the election had not even taken place for all the effect it had on the government. The military rulers said it was not safe to pass power to civilians at this time. They declared, "We cannot say for how long we will be in charge of the state administration. It might be five years or ten."[4]

Some NLD activists fled to Manerplaw, an area just across the Thailand border. *Manerplaw* means "victory place," and a wooden arch there proclaims the brave words of American patriot Patrick Henry: "Give me liberty or give me death!" Some of the men fighting for democracy in Manerplaw are the sons and grandsons of the brave men who drove out the Japanese invaders during World War II. They live in bamboo and hardwood stilt buildings, and during the rainy season, the entire place seems to wash away.[5]

The government has tried to undermine Suu Kyi's prestige throughout her house arrest. The rulers cite her marriage to an Englishman as proof of her loyalty to a foreign government. But to most Burmese people, especially since the 1990 election, she is regarded as the legal ruler of the country. Her picture is found all over Burma on illegal posters and buttons. Her style of dress, a combination of traditional and western, has been adopted by many young people in the country.

In October 1991 Suu Kyi was chosen to receive the Nobel Peace Prize. Her husband was living at the time in Cambridge, Massachusetts (as a visiting professor at Harvard University). Neither he nor the children had accompanied Suu Kyi when she returned to Burma. At this point Aris had not seen his wife in two years.[6] He reacted to the news of her award with "great emotion, great joy and pride and also sadness and continued apprehension about her situation."[7]

In giving Suu Kyi the prize, the Nobel Prize Committee said they were honoring her "to show respect for the many people throughout the world who are striving to attain democracy, human rights, and ethnic conciliation by peaceful measures." The committee added, "Suu Kyi's struggle is one of the most extraordinary examples of civil courage in Asia in recent decades."[8]

Roger Clark of Canada's Amnesty International called the Burmese woman's selection valuable in calling attention to the plight of political prisoners in the country. "More publicity is more security for most prisoners of conscience,"[9] he said.

Accepting the award for Suu Kyi, eighteen-year-old Alexander said the award belonged not only to his mother, but to all the men, women, and children who struggled for a democratic Burma. Alexander was joined by his fourteen-year-old brother, Kim, and their father in Oslo.

Within Burma, the struggle continues. Burmese citizens are routinely picked up to work for the army. And anyone who publicly protests is in great peril of vanishing without a trace.

There are numerous trouble spots around the world, and the agony of the once "Golden Land" continues without much of a world outcry. There are even some in Asia who were offended by the choice of Suu Kyi as a Nobel Prize winner. These people saw her selection as a form of interference in their internal affairs. One Asian diplomat shrugged the prize off as a "non-event."[10] In the meantime many countries in the region are eager to trade the teak and minerals Burma offers for the armaments Burma desires.

Suu Kyi remained under house arrest in 1993—forbidden to send or receive letters, telephone calls, or any communication with the outside world. There were indications that she may be considering a hunger strike in an effort to force the government to negotiate with her for the release of political prisoners and the restoration of some form of democracy in the country. Her captors have told her that she can be free only if she accepts permanent foreign exile, and this she will not do.

On a soldier's tomb in the outpost at Maner-plaw, the words of the American patriot Nathan Hale, are scrawled: "I only regret that I have but one life to lose for my country." Friends of Burmese democracy and those who love and admire Nobel Laureate Suu Kyi hope that her life will not be another one lost in the struggle for freedom.

Rigoberta Menchu

Rigoberta Menchu
To Share the Dream of Peace

When Rigoberta Menchu was only eight, she began to work at her mother's side picking coffee beans on a Guatemalan plantation. She picked about twenty-eight pounds of coffee beans a day in the hot sun. Often she would glance at her mother Juana Tum, who carried her baby brother Nicolas, in a shawl on her back. Juana Tum's face dripped with perspiration as she picked the beans from the bushes and ground.

Rigoberta's older brother Felipe, had already died after a plane sprayed pesticides on the field where he worked. Now baby Nicolas cried all the time, and his stomach was swollen with malnutrition.

Early one morning Nicolas died. There had been no money for food or medicine. Juana Tum could not afford to buy a burial spot so she could not even bury her baby. Finally a friend brought a little box to use as a coffin and loaned the family money for the burial. But afterward the landowner Rigoberta and her mother worked for was so furious they had taken time off that he fired them. Somehow they made their way back to the mountainous region where they lived.

Rigoberta Menchu, a Maya-Quiché Indian, was born in 1959 in the hamlet of Chimel. Chimel is near San Miguel de Upsantán, capital of the north-western province of El Quiché in Guatemala. Rigoberta never attended school. Her family lived four months of each year in the mountains and then traveled down to the coast to pick coffee beans or cotton. By the time Rigoberta was ten she could pick forty pounds of coffee beans in a day. She could also chop heavy undergrowth with a machete beside her father, Vicente Menchu.

At the age of ten, the girls in Rigoberta Menchu's tribe were considered adults with serious duties. At this age Menchu took part in a ceremony where she promised to serve the community. When twelve years old, she received two small chickens and a lamb to symbolize her growing importance in the family and community. She helped harvest the maize in the mountains and took part in deciding whether to plant potatoes or beans. At this time Menchu also became a catechist in the Catholic Church. A catechist's duties include giving religious instruction to children, leading prayer services when a priest is not available to say mass, and guiding the spiritual development of the community.

After leading prayer services, Menchu held discussions on how the community could improve its harsh living conditions. She began clearly to see how injustices in society made life harder for her people. She talked about going to the capital to ask the government to improve living conditions for the Indian people in the mountains and throughout Guatemala. Menchu saw that the rights of labor were not respected, that most of the land was owned by a few people, and that the Indian children had no opportunity to go to school. She became determined to play a role in correcting these abuses.

When Menchu was fourteen she and her close friend, Maria, were picking cotton in a field. Like Menchu, the other girl was also a catechist with a fine mind and strong ambition. Suddenly planes appeared overhead, spraying pesticides onto the field. Maria grew desperately ill and soon died. Menchu said she had to struggle with hatred against people who would spray poison on human beings working in a field.[1]

When an older teenager, Menchu went to the capital to work as a maid in a rich man's house. Her father opposed her decision because he feared she'd be mistreated, and all alone in the city, she'd have no one to turn to. Unfortunately his fears came true as Menchu and the other servants were given only a few beans and hard tortillas to eat. Even the dogs owned by the family received better food.

The sons of the wealthy household would throw their dirty dishes in the faces of the maids, and the mistress of the family complained if she found a speck of dust on the furniture. Menchu and her fellow servants hurried to bring trays of food to members of the household reclining in bed, shouting their demands. When Menchu's father came to visit her, he was not even allowed inside the house. He looked so poor and dirty that he had to visit his daughter in the yard.

Vicente Menchu had a bitter childhood himself. Orphaned as a boy, he was forced to run errands for a wealthy family who refused the boy even a place inside to sleep at night. He had to live with the animals, always cold, hungry, and filthy. In his late teens he was forced into the army.[2]

In the late 1970s, large landowners—with government support—began to take over farmland in Rigoberta Menchu's village. This land had been used to provide subsistence farming for many generations. Since this was the only way for the poor farmers to survive, they began to resist the land takeover. Vicente Menchu joined the *Comite Unidad Campesino* (CUC), or Committee for Campesino Unity, to defend the peasants' land.

Vicente Menchu became a hero among his neighbors, fighting for laws to protect Indian land. But hired henchmen of the angry landowners savagely beat him. Rigoberta Menchu and her family found him lying tortured and abandoned by the roadside, the hair on one side of his head torn off. He was almost dead when they took him to a hospital. The landowners threatened to kidnap Vicente from the hospital bed so, with the help of local priests and nuns, he was spirited off to a secret place and nursed back to health.

Menchu now worked full time in the crusade to bring land reform, carrying on her father's work. Once Menchu and her *compañeros* (companions) stood watch in a village so they could warn others if soldiers came. One soldier stumbled into a trap and he was now at the mercy of the compañeros. He was just a young man and he said he had been forced into the army and ordered to attack villages against his will. Menchu and her companions set him free when he promised never again to attack the poor people of Guatemala. In spite of all the misery and cruelty she'd seen, Menchu remained compassionate.

Petrona Chona, mother of two small children, was Menchu's friend. One day the son of a landowner came to demand that she be his mistress. When Chona refused, thugs sent by the landowner's son cut her to pieces with machetes. Chona's children witnessed her brutal death, and Menchu herself saw the mutilated body of her friend. The horrifying sight left Menchu with recurring nightmares for the next six years.[3] When the murderer was caught, he was punished with just fifteen days in jail, a tragic example of how lightly authorities took the lives of the peasants.

In 1978, when Menchu was nineteen years old, terrible murders and rapes ravaged the villages of Guatemala. Menchu was already a marked woman because of her political activities and she traveled constantly to avoid capture. Nuns taught her to read and write during the long periods she hid in convents.

In the spring of 1978, oil was discovered on peasant land in Panzós. The peasants were ordered off the land, but they had nowhere else to go. So they organized a protest and refused to move. On May 29, 1978, the army massacred 106 men, women, and children—mostly Indians. Blood ran like rainwater in the city square.

After the massacre at Panzós, the CUC doubled its efforts. The organization demanded fair wages, respect for the communities, and decent treatment for all people. It called for strikes and demonstrations, sometimes gaining concessions from landowners. But frequently the landowners' promises were broken. Menchu was now busy learning other Indian languages as well as Spanish so she could be more effective. She carried papers, printing machines, leaflets, and teaching texts from village to village.

In September 1979 Petrocino Menchu, Rigoberta Menchu's sixteen-year-old brother was kidnapped. A catechist, he was found with a Bible and other religious texts. His captors, already very suspicious of the role the Catholic Church was playing among poor people, decided that the boy's possession of these materials meant he was a communist stirring up the people against the government.

Petrocino Menchu was brutally beaten and his clothing ripped off. He was tortured in an effort to make him give evidence against the priests in the villages. The priests were already suspected of being communists because they helped organize the peasants. For sixteen days the boy was tortured, after which time he was thrown into the street.

When Menchu and her mother arrived on the scene they could not even recognize the bruised and bleeding face of Petrocino. Both Menchu and her mother watched helplessly as the dying boy, along with other peasant captives, were drenched with gasoline and set afire. Soldiers roared with laughter as the prisoners were burned alive. Juana Tum, Menchu's mother, half dead with grief, crept forward at last to kiss the burned body of her son. Then the family took the charred remains away for burial.

Still the Menchu family continued struggling for justice. Now recovered from his own injuries, Vicente Menchu again took a leadership role in the CUC. He said, "I am a Christian and the duty of a Christian is to fight all the injustices committed against our people."[4] The people now meant not only the indigenous Indian population, but all the poor of Guatemala, regardless of their ethnic background.

During a large demonstration that included students, workers, and peasants, Vicente Menchu and others occupied the Spanish Embassy. On January 31, 1980, a peaceful sit-in at the embassy began in Guatemala City. The protesters vowed to remain in the embassy until there was some resolution to the problem of land seizures in the Indian highlands and an end to massacres in peasant villages. The national police set fire to the embassy to drive out the protestors and Vicente Menchu was burned alive with thirty-eight other peasant farmers.[5]

Menchu had now lost four close family members, but the twenty-year-old became even more active in the CUC. She said, "My commitment to our struggle recognizes neither boundaries nor limits; only those of us who carry our cause in our hearts are ready to run the risks."[6] Menchu had a dream in which her dead father encouraged her to keep the struggle going.

Now in the village where Menchu lived, the people were so frightened of the army that they dared not even go to the store for supplies. Menchu missed her father deeply but she said, "we must prevail over the times we are living in with the help of our ancestors."[7]

Juana Tum had long been under suspicion as the wife of Vicente Menchu. One day she was kidnapped and placed under arrest by the army. While in captivity, she was raped and beaten by army officers. After many days of starvation and torture, the bleeding and disfigured woman was taken to a field and left to die. For several days she lay there, too weak to move until her body was covered with worms. Animals from the surrounding hills came to attack her, and she died in terrible agony.

The grief that her mother's death inflicted on Menchu was almost unbearable. She had now lost both parents to savage cruelty and seen her young brother burned to death. She had also lost two other brothers to malnutrition and poisoning. Though just twenty years old, Menchu had witnessed more horror than most battle-hardened veterans in a long lifetime.

In January 1981 Menchu joined a popular front to commemorate the massacre of her father and the others at the Spanish Embassy. The group organized boycotts and loosed "propaganda bombs," which were leaflets promoting its cause. The government now set out to capture Menchu, and it almost succeeded. One day she'd taken refuge in a church, and as the soldiers surged in, she let her long hair fall over her face and bent low in prayer. Miraculously, they missed her, but finally Menchu had to admit she could not stay in Guatemala. In 1981 she took a plane to Mexico, but she was determined not to abandon the cause of her people.

In 1983, with the help of a friend, Menchu

wrote a book titled *I, Rigoberta Menchu: An Indian Woman in Guatemala.* In the book the twenty-three-year-old woman described the sad and shocking events of her life in a way that made it clear that many others were suffering as she had, without world notice. Menchu's book seized the attention of people all over the world.

Menchu became a founding member of the Unified Representation of the Guatemala Opposition (RUOG), a group of exiled Guatemalan leaders working to publicize the cause of the peasants to the world community. Menchu also joined many international groups, including the United Nations (UN) working group on indigenous peoples and the UN subcommission on the prevention of discrimination and the protection of minorities. She had been a credentialed observer of the UN General Assembly and the Commission on Human Rights.[8]

In May 1988 Menchu attempted to return to Guatemala to take part in talks on land reform. The Catholic bishops of Guatemala had issued a pastoral letter demanding that the needs of the peasants be confronted in a just manner. Menchu, now head of the CUC, called the pastoral letter an important step in bringing a solution to the country's most pressing problem—land reform. She was arrested, however, when she landed in the country, and only pressure from the world forced her release back into exile.

A year later Menchu made another attempt to return to her country, but death threats drove her

Despite the many tragedies that have occurred during her life, Rigoberta Menchu continues to fight for the rights of the poor in Guatemala.

back. In July 1992 Menchu managed at last to return to Guatemala under the protection of international representatives. The humble young woman was received as a heroine by the peasants of her country who saw in her someone who would speak for them before the world.

In October 1992 Rigoberta Menchu was chosen to win the Nobel Peace Prize as a spokesperson for the indigenous people of Guatemala. The Nobel Prize Committee, in giving Menchu the prize, condemned the "large-scale repression of Indian peoples" in Guatemala in the 1970s and 1980s.

Menchu said, "I am very hopeful that this will help the Indian people of the Americas live on forever."[9] She then added, "I wish my dear father, Vicente Menchu, and mother, Juana Tum, were here to share the dream of peace of the Guatemalan people."[10] Menchu promised to use the Nobel Peace Prize money to further her work for the Guatemalan Indians.

In January 1993, ending ten years of exile, twenty-four hundred Guatemalans left Mexico, traveling in a caravan back to their homeland. They were welcomed home by Rigoberta Menchu, who called the return "a symbol of hope for those who are left behind."[11]

Menchu herself has become a shining symbol of hope. For the some 87 percent of her people who continue to live in poverty, her Nobel Peace Prize has shed light on the sufferings of people too long in darkness.

Chapter Notes

Chapter 1

1. Bertha Kinsky, *Lay Down Your Arms*, English trans. (London: Longmans Green, 1895), p. 1.

2. Tony Gray, *Champions of Peace* (Birmingham: Paddington Press, Ltd., 1976), p. 88.

3. Ibid.

4. Ibid. p. 90.

5. Bertha von Suttner, *Memoirs*, Vol. II (New York: Ginn, 1910), p. 4.

6. Gray, p. 89.

7. Ibid.

8. Von Suttner, *Memoirs*, p. 5.

9. Gray, p. 89.

10. Bertha von Suttner, Nobel Prize address delivered to the Norwegian Nobel Institute, Oslo, Norway, 1906.

11. Von Suttner, *Memoirs*, p. 4.

12. Gray, p. 88.

Chapter 2

1. Allen F. Davis, *American Heroine, The Life and Legend of Jane Addams* (New York: Oxford University Press, 1973), p. 223.

2. Ibid.

3. Jane Addams, *Twenty Years at Hull House* (New York: Macmillan, 1935), p. 117.

4. Davis, p. 225.

5. Jane Addams, *The Spirit of Youth and the City Streets* (New York: Macmillan, 1910), p. 24.

6. Davis, p. 226.

7. Addams, *Twenty Years at Hull House,* p. 117.

8. George E. Mowry, *Theodore Roosevelt and the Progressive Movement* (New York: Hill & Wang, 1946); and Theodore Roosevelt, *Roosevelt MSS*, Library of Congress (Roosevelt letter to Henry Green, July 2, 1915).

9. Davis, p. 291.

10. Ibid.

11. Robert Murray, *The Red Scare: A Study in National Hysteria 1919–1920* (Minneapolis: University of Minnesota Press, 1955), p. 200.

12. Walter Lippman, column, *Los Angeles Times* (May 23, 1935) p. 6.

Chapter 3

1. Walter Millis, "Road to War," *America, 1914–1917. The Historians History of the United States*, Vol. II (New York: G.P. Putnams Sons, 1966), p. 1156.

2. Ibid. p. 1151.

3. Mercedes M. Randall, *Improper Bostonian* (New York: Twayne Pub. Inc., 1964), p. 224.

4. Ibid. p. 228.

5. Emily Greene Balch, *Our Slavic Fellow Citizens* (New York: Charities Pub. Co., 1910), p. 425.

6. Ibid. p. 419.

7. John Herman Randall, *Emily Green Balch of New England: Citizen of the World* (Washington D.C.: Womens International League for Peace and Freedom, 1940), p. 200.

8. Emily Greene Balch, Nobel Prize address delivered to the Norwegian Nobel Institute, Oslo, Norway, 1946.

Chapter 4

1. Mairead Corrigan Maguire, "A Peaceful Planet: Every Child's Birthright," *Pax Christi Bulletin* (Fall 1990), p. 6.

2. Richard Deutsch, *Mairead Corrigan/Betty Williams*, trans. Jack Bernard (New York: Barrons, 1977), p. 4.

3. Ibid. p. 6.

4. Ibid. p. 60.

5. Ibid. p. 121.

6. "Price of Peace," pamphlet of the Peace People, 1976.

7. Gerry Adams, "Peace in Ireland," pamphlet (Belfast Republican Press Center, 1976).

8. BBC appearance of Rev. Ian Paisley, September 14, 1976.

9. *The Protestant Telegraph*, October, 1976, No. 7, Vol. II, p. 1.

10. Model Constitution of the Peace People, January 7, 1977.

11. Deutsch, p. 194.

12. Ibid. p. 196.

13. Mairead Corrigan Maguire, excerpts from keynote address delivered to Pax Christi USA National Assembly, August 3–5, at Canisius College, Buffalo, N.Y., 1990.

14. Ibid.

Chapter 5

1. Malcolm Muggeridge, *Something Beautiful for God: Mother Teresa of Calcutta* (London: Collins, 1971), p. 49.

2. Robert Serrou, *Teresa of Calcutta* (New York: McGraw-Hill Book Co., 1980), p. 26.

3. Ibid. p. 24.

4. Mother Teresa, "Gospel of Five Fingers," *Mission Magazine* (Summer 1991), p. 6.

5. Constitution of the International Association of Co-workers of Mother Teresa affiliated to the Missionaries of Charity, October 7, 1950.

6. Ibid.

7. Gigi Colson, "Calcutta Through the Eye of the Needle," *Liguorian* (July 1993), p. 62.

8. Serrou, p. 48.

9. Ibid. p. 50.

10. Colson, p. 59.

11. Mother Teresa, Nobel Prize address delivered to the Norwegian Nobel Institute, Oslo, Norway, December 10, 1979.

12. Ibid.

13. Professor John Sanness, Chairman of Nobel Committee, speech delivered on occasion of award of Peace Prize, December 10, 1979.

14. Mother Teresa, Nobel Prize address.

15. "Mother Teresa Wins Nobel," *The Washington Post* (October 20, 1979), p. 1.

16. Mother Teresa, Nobel Prize address.

Chapter 6

1. President John F. Kennedy, televised speech of October 22, 1962.

2. Sissela Bok, *Alva Myrdal: A Daughter's Memoir* (Reading, Mass.: Addison Wellesley, 1991), p. 20.

3. "Newsletter," Department of Public Information of the United Nations (Lake Success, N.Y., February 1949), p. 1.

4. "Newsletter," Department of Public Information of the United Nations (Lake Success, N.Y., 1950), p. 1.

5. Alva Myrdal, et al., *Dynamics of European Nuclear Disarmament* (London: Spokesmen Ltd., 1982), p. 5.

6. United Nations Document (New York, January 1964), p. 1.

7. Alva Myrdal, *The Game of Disarmament: How the United States and Russia Run the Arms Race* (London: Spokesmen Ltd., 1976), p. 1.

Chapter 7

1. Fergus M. Bordewich, "Rape of the Golden Land," *Readers Digest* (December 1991), p. 131.

2. Ibid.

3. Ibid.

4. James D. Ross, "Rain of Terror," *The New Republic* (October 28, 1991), p. 12.

5. Ibid. p. 10.

6. Diane Brady, "A Fight for Rights," *MacLeans* (October 28, 1991), p. 84.

7. Ibid.

8. Bruce W. Nelan, "Heroine in Chains," *Time* (October 28, 1991), p. 73.

9. Brady, p. 84.

10. Nelan, p. 73.

Chapter 8

1. Rigoberta Menchu, *I, Rigoberta Menchu: An Indian Woman in Guatemala,* ed. Elisabeth Burgos Debray and trans. Ann Wright (Norfolk, Va.: Thetford Press Ltd., 1984), p. 89.

2. Ibid. p. 3.

3. Ibid. p. 152.

4. Ibid. p. 183.

5. Greg Erlandson, ed., "Catholic Rights Activist Wins Nobel Prize," *Our Sunday Visitor* (October 25, 1992), p. 4.

6. Menchu, p. 244.

7. Ibid. p. 195.

8. Newsletter of Network in Solidarity With the People of Guatemala (October 1992), p. 1.

9. Stella Bugge, "Indians and Nobel Is Reply to Columbus," *San Diego Union* (October 16, 1992), p. 1.

10. Ibid. p. 16.

11. Lynne Walker, "Caravan of Hope," *San Diego Union Tribune* (January 21, 1993), p. A22.

Index

A

Addams, Jane, 21–33, 40, 41
Addams, John Huy, 21–22
American Dilemma, An, 76
Aris, Michael, 84
Aung San, General, 84

B

Balch, Emily, 35–45
Boers, 13
Bryn Mawr College, 37–38
Butler, Nicholas Murray, 32

C

Carnegie Endowment for
    Peace, 17
Carter, Jimmy, 68
Committee for Campesino
    Unity, 96–98
Corrigan, Mairead, 47–57
Cuban Missile Crisis, 72

D

Denison House, 37–39
Dunant, Jean Henry, 16

F

Francis Ferdinand, Archduke,
    18
Franco-Prussian War, 9

G

Gandhi, Indira, 68

H

Hague Peace Conference,
    First, 15

Hague Peace Conference,
    Second, 17
Hale, Nathan, 91
Hapsburg throne, 18
Henry, Patrick, 88
Hitler, Adolf, 44
Hull House, 23, 32

I

International Congress of
    Women for Permanent
    Peace, 28, 41
Irish Republican Army, 48,
    51, 53, 54

J

Japanese Americans, 44–45

K

Kennedy, John F., 71–72

L

Lay Down Your Arms, 9, 12
League of Nations, 44
Lippman, Walter, 32–33
Lusk Committee, 30

M

Machine Age, The, 12
Maguire, Anne, 47–48
McKinley, William, 25
Menchu, Petrocino, 98–99
Menchu, Rigoberta, 93–103
Menchu, Vicente, 99–100
Missionaries of Charity, 62
Myrdal, Alva, 71–81
Myrdal, Gunnar, 74, 76, 78

N

Ne Win, U, 86
Nicholas II, Czar, 15
Nobel, Alfred, 10, 11, 19
Noordam, 41

O

Oscar II, 41
Ottoman Empire, 11

P

Paisley, Ian, 53
Pax Christi USA, 55
Peace People, 53, 54

R

Rankin, Jeanette, 36
Reagan, Ronald, 68, 79–80
Riksdag, 78
Roosevelt, Theodore, 26–28
Russo-Turkish Wars, 11–13

S

Sanness, John, 66
Saw Maung, General, 88
Schurz, Carl, 25
Shantinagar, 64
Sisters of Loreto, 61
Spanish-American War, 15, 39
Starr, Helen Gates, 23
Stockholm International Peace Research Institute, 79

Suu Kyi, Daw Aung Sun, 82–91

T

Tatmadaw, 84
Teresa, Mother, 59–69, 57
Thant, U, 79
Tolstoy, Leo, 25
Tum, Juana, 93, 100, 101, 104
Twenty Years at Hull House, 26

U

Uncle Tom's Cabin, 9
Unified Representation of the Guatemalan Opposition, 102

V

Von Kinsky, Franz Joseph, 10
Von Suttner, Bertha, 9–19
Von Suttner, Arthur Gundaccar, 10

W

Wellesley College, 39, 43–44
Williams, Betty, 47–57
Wilson, Woodrow, 30
Women's International League for Peace and Freedom, 32, 44
World War I, 18–19, 26–30